SIGN OF TIMES

A Music Anthology with Lyric Analysis

JULEON SCHINS

Sign of Times:
A Music Anthology with Lyric Analysis

© 2019 by Juleon Schins. All rights reserved.

No part of this publication may be reproduced, stored in a retrieval system or transmitted in any way by any means, electronic, mechanical, photocopy, recording or otherwise without the prior permission of the author except as provided by US copyright law.

ISBN 978-1-64550-006-3   (Paperback)

Contents

Introduction	Sign of Times	i
Chapter 1	Bryan Adams	1
Chapter 2	Paul McCartney	9
Chapter 3	Mick Jagger	17
Chapter 4	Paul Simon	21
Chapter 5	Björn and Benny	25
Chapter 6	Sting	29
Chapter 7	Bono	33
Chapter 8	Roger Waters	37
Chapter 9	Freddie Mercury	43
Chapter 10	Mark Knopfler	51
Chapter 11	Don Henley	57
Chapter 12	Michael Stipes	63
Chapter 13	Phil Collins	69
Chapter 14	Eric Clapton	75
Chapter 15	Bruce Springsteen	81
Chapter 16	Robert Plant	85

This book is part of a 2019 decalogue consisting of

- Sign of Times: Music Anthology and Lyric Analysis
- Hollywood Misogyny
- Beginners' Guide to the FED:
  Why it is Unique on our Planet
- The Kennedy Kurse: Four Obvious Konnektions
- Manichaeism and Satanic Child Abuse
- Progressive Intolerance: Last Stop Before Hitler
- Patriotic Ingenuousness
- Deism versus Theism:
  2-7 in the Scientific Arena of the 20th Century
- Feminine Feminist:
  A Missing Link Eluding Discovery
- The Snake: Three Millennia of Anti-Semitism

Dedicated to Annique

INTRODUCTION
Sign of Times

Music is a cultural expression, like every other human art. From every piece of art, a specialist is able to guess what kind of society such a piece of art belongs to, and what the specific sentiments or message of the artists are. The most important aspect of a culture, generally speaking, is its moral level, because it is immediately connected to the survival odds of a society. Hence, the music is the expression of the "Darwinist fitness" of a society, too. One might ask: why morality? Why not average wealth, average life expectancy, or technological level?

History will tell us. The best studied example of rise and fall of a culture is the ancient Roman one. Emperor Hadrian built a defensive wall splitting England in two. His predecessors called the Mediterranean "mare nostrum" (our sea), because they controlled all countries around it: the contemporary North Africa, Israel, Turkey, Greece, Albania, Italy, France, and Spain, as well as Switzerland, Germany, and the Netherlands. St. Augustine already wrote in detail why the Western Roman Empire fell as a dead leaf: not because of lack of wealth, life expectancy, or technological level, but because the ruling class was morally degenerated. Who has not heard of roman parties, where participants induced their own vomiting in order to be able to continue eating? The role of women in such parties one can imagine without too many efforts. Do you know of a single Roman woman who made it to the senate? Their status was the same in all previous cultures: being property of a man. Christianity, which had a totally different concept of the role of woman in society, did not cause the fall of Rome, it merely witnessed it. During three centuries they were brutally butchered in Roman stadia, which is hardly a sign of Christian domination. That the SPQR even enjoyed watching the ruthless murder of plenty of innocent people, is nothing but a sign of moral degeneration.

Today, like in ancient Roman times, western civilization is about to collapse. Again, this is due to our steady loss of morality. The following are decidedly signs of moral degeneration:

- the exponential increase of family-imposed euthanasia's and of boyfriend-imposed abortions;
- a decrease in the quality of parent-child relationship;
- the universal plague of ritual child offerings, like in nearly all ancient civilizations;
- a steady rise of adult women trade, which grows increasingly faster than the population itself.

People sometimes wonder about the "brutality of the Middle Ages".

First, one has to know when they started (with the fall of the Roman Empire, which is different for Eastern and Western Europe), and when they ended (with the Italian renaissance in the West). Instead of contemplating that brutality in the context of contemporaneity, one should compare the status of society at the beginning and the end of those Middle Ages. *The difference is so enormous that one cannot identify a single other culture that even approaches such a social advancement in so short a time.* After the Middle Ages came Enlightenment, supposedly "to break us loose from the shackles of Christianity", but practically, to turn back the clock of personal freedom by one millennium. Obviously, peasants who believe in their freedom are more difficult to handle than peasants who believe they are slaves.

Burning witches at the stake is an invention of obscurantism, too. That retrograde ideology falsely attributed such practices to the Catholic Church. This mostly happened in theocracies, in general: A social solution which Christ Himself had already condemned when He said "give to the Caesar what is Ceasar's, and to God what is God's." Protestantism never noticed this extreme inconsistency, especially Calvinism.

Machiavellian politics is another invention of obscurantism. Voltaire's publicly vomiting over the Catholic Church ("écrasez l'infâme"), is a typical expression of obscurantism, too. Systematic stealing[1]

---

1 All property of the Church was always due to donations by its faithful. The Catholic Church never robbed a single piece of art, unlike the filthy rat Napoleon, who managed himself alone to fill the Louvre with nothing but stolen art. I never heard a single Frenchman complaining about that, including

property of the Catholic Church, usually justified "in order to sustain the poor", though in practice ending up in the pockets of the parvenu bourgeois, was eminently obscurantist, too. The only positive achievement of obscurantism is that it definitively removed the clergy from the "Assemblée Nationale", where clergy has nothing to seek in the first place. The fight between today's obscurantism and Christianity is still going on, and shall no doubt continue, until the end of times.

In this book I do not propose any specific policies against societal degeneration, nor against mafias and freemasonries. I only present sixteen top-100 songs, whose lyrics appropriately mirror the morality our western societies. This mirror view I call "Sign of Times", as it has a quite predictable extrapolation to the future.

As a rule, for better legibility, **all quoted passages are written in a different font** as compared to the standard.

---

the very orthodox Catholic ones. I did hear of the very opposite: of graciously pious Catholics lighting their candles to Saint Napoleon. That is a quite neat example of patriotism-induced blindness and stupidity.

Chapter 1
Bryan Adams

I present to you a Canadian father of two children, once and still married (to Alicia Grimaldi, 2009), with eminently *positive* lyrics. Bryan writes about sacrifice and giving one's life for one's beloved. He has so many philanthropic activities that one can hardly sum them up.[2]

---

[2] Here follow just four hands full:
- own foundation aims to advance education and learning opportunities for children and young people worldwide, believing that an education is the best gift that a child can be given;
- his first high-profile charity appearance came in 1985 when he opened the US transmission of Live Aid from Philadelphia;
- in June of the next year, Adams participated in the two-week Amnesty International "A Conspiracy of Hope" tour alongside Sting, U2 and Peter Gabriel;
- in 1986, Adams performed at The Prince's Trust All-Star Rock Concert in Wembley Arena to celebrate first 10 years of the Trust and again in June 1987 at the 5th Annual Prince's Trust Rock Gala along with Elton John, George Harrison, Ringo Starr and others;
- the following year Adams performed at the Nelson Mandela birthday party concert at Wembley Stadium;

- he commemorated the fall of the Berlin Wall when, in 1990, he joined many other guests for Roger Waters' massive performance of The Wall in Berlin, Germany;
- he joined the CBC benefit concert in Toronto for victims of the 2004 Indian Ocean earthquake;
- twenty years after performing at Live Aid in the US, Adams played at Canada's Live 8 show in Barrie, Ontario;
- he performed in Qatar and raised UK£1.5M (US$2,617,000) from the concert;
- he also auctioned a white Fender Stratocaster guitar signed by prominent guitarists, which raised a total of US$3.7 million for charity; the money went to Qatar's "Reach Out to Asia" campaign to help the underprivileged across the continent;
- his own projects are more specific: rebuilding a school in Thailand and building a new sports center in Sri Lanka, both of which had been devastated by the Indian Ocean tsunami
- on 25 May 2005, Adams raised £1.3M with cousin Johnny Armitage, from a concert and auction entitled Rock by the River for the Royal Marsden Hospital in London;
- on 15 May 2006, Adams returned to London to attend the Hope Foundation's event (hosted by designer Bella Freud), helping to raise a portion of the £250,000 to support the Palestinian refugee children;
- the following June, he offered individuals from the public the chance to bid to sing with him live in concert at three different charity auctions in London;
- over £50,000 was raised with money going to the NSPCC, Children in Need, and the University College Hospital;
- on 28 February 2008 he appeared in One Night Live at the Air Canada Centre in Toronto, Ontario, Canada with Josh Groban, Sarah McLachlan, Jann Arden and RyanDan in aid of the Sunnybrook Hospital Women and Babies Program;

This list marks the stature of a man with uncountable talents; yet a man who uses those talents not to fill his pockets, but to help reducing misery in our world.

The tune love-song tune is quite beyond average, with an excellent band coverage: it is very soft and distant-sounding when Bryan sings, and opens all channels to full decibels when he's done singing. On the podium you won't catch Bryan trying to concentrate all attraction on himself, nor ostensibly pointing out his gratitude to the band members accompanying him. This humility is easily recognized in the official clip, too: the first shots show people jumping over the fences, or storming onto the field when the fences are officially opened to the public; to his distant, over-the-top (I guess ironically meant) semi-

- on 29 January 2006, Adams became the first Western artist to perform in Karachi, Pakistan, after 11 September attacks, in conjunction with a benefit concert by Shehzad Roy to raise money for underprivileged children to go to school;
- on 18 October 2007, Adams was billed to perform in Tel Aviv and Jericho as part of the OneVoice Movement concerts, hoping to aid in solving the Israeli–Palestinian conflict; the peace concert for supporters of a two-state solution to the conflict with Israel was called off because of security concerns (read: because of EZ's repulsion for Palestinians);
- he supports the *Hear the World* initiative as a photographer in its aim to raise global awareness for the topic of hearing and hearing loss;
- he published a photography book entitled *Wounded – The Legacy of War* (2013) to highlight the human consequences of war; he also recorded songs critical of warfare on past albums.

presidential limousine parade, without however showing his face in the most important limousine; and finally, to the body-builders putting together his platform like if it were a children's puzzle. Only then, long after his podium appearance has started. does the camera zoom in on him. His live actuation on the podium is continually interrupted by short footages of his daily life with colleagues and friends, as far as the preparations of a live presentation is concerned. Just as modest is his taking leave from the public after his song: no repeated bows, but a simple blink of the eye and turn around.

As far as the lyrics are concerned, they are not the usual the usual vulgar allusions to having sex. He tells his beloved "I can't help it, there's nothing I want more", *referring to her trying to look into her heart, in her soul.* That is, he declares his love by everything he would do for her: lying, walking the wire, giving everything, even his life; however, he clearly challenges her to look into her heart, in order to find himself. His is not a stupid, unconditional love: no, it is a free love, self-willed, but on the condition that it be corresponded by the beloved.

Chapeau!

I Do It for You
Adams, Lange, and Kamen[3]

Look into my eyes, you will see
What you mean to me
Search your heart search your soul
And when you find me there,
you'll search no more
Don't tell me it's not worth tryin' for
You can't tell me it's not worth dyin' for
You know it's true
Everything I do, I do it for you
Look into your heart, you will find
There's nothin' there to hide
Take me as I am, take my life
I would give it all, I would sacrifice
Don't tell me it's not worth fightin' for
I can't help it, there's nothin' I want more
You know it's true
Everything I do, I do it for you

---

[3] (Everything I Do) I Do It for You lyrics © Universal Music Publishing Group, Vintage House Publishing

There's no love like your love
And no other could give more love
There's nowhere unless you're there
All the time, all the way, yeah
You can't tell me it's not worth tryin' for
I can't help it there's nothin' I want more
Yeah, I would fight for you, I lie for you
Walk the wire for you,
yeah, I'd die for you
You know it's true
Everything I do, I do it for you
Look into your heart
You can't tell me it ain't worth dying for
I'll be there, yeah
I'll walk the wire for you
I will die for you

Bryan Adams

Although Bryan Adams has a quite limited lyrical repertoire (all his songs are about love), he no doubt merits a statue for his unprecedented talent to drive a mega-sized public collectively out of its mind with the sound of only his guitar, very gently and parsimoniously used, and his, for opera standards quite modest, but beautiful, hoarse voice.

CHAPTER 2
Paul McCartney

After a long period of touring, the Beatles were on the edge of falling apart. Since the "excellent influence" of Bob Dylan led to their addiction to LSD, the group suffered increasingly of internal strains. Things really got out of hand in 1969 when Yoko suffered a miscarriage, following a drug bust the month before. Lennon's bad habitude to bring his wife along in the studio only increased the internal friction. It seemed very much an end of the Beatles. Thanks so much, Bob. Better stick to your own business in the future.

The initiative to start playing live again, after years of play-back on Beatlemania tours, was Paul's. He proposed a crucial decoy: the "back to basics" idea, which meant importantly reducing the high-tech artifice added by the producers to their songs. The idea was well accepted by all band members, although the band's falling apart was not miraculously solved.

As usual, Paul and John were co-authors of most of their songs. The tune and lyrics of "Let it be" are clearly Paul's, though. He said how this song came about in a unique way, different from all his other songs: by his own mum (ten year dead at that time) speaking to him in a dream.

Let It Be happened during a time when there was kind of a lot going on. I think people were overdoing the use of substances. We certainly were. It was kind of common. It was the fashion. And anyone who remembers that time will know that. And I think I was getting, like, a little bit over the top with the whole thing – getting pretty tired and pretty wasted. And I went to bed one night and had a kind of restless night. But I had a dream where my mother, who had been dead at that point for about 10 years, came to me in the dream and it was as if she could see that I was troubled. And she sort of said to me, she said, 'Let it be.' And I remember quite clearly her saying ,'Let it be,' and 'It's going to be OK. Don't worry.' You know, 'Let it be.' I woke up and I remembered the dream, and I thought, 'Well, that's a great idea.' And I then sat down and wrote the song using the feeling from that dream and of my mum coming to me in the dream.

Let It Be (Beatles)
Lennon and McCartney[4]

When I find myself in times of trouble,
Mother Mary comes to me
Speaking words of wisdom, let it be
And in my hour of darkness
she is standing right in front of me
Speaking words of wisdom, let it be
Ref: Let it be (3x),
Whisper words of wisdom, let it be
And when the broken hearted people living in the world agree
There will be an answer, let it be
For though they may be parted,
there is still a chance that they will see
There will be an answer, let it be [Ref]
And when the night is cloudy there is still a light that shines on me
Shine until tomorrow, let it be
I wake up to the sound of music,
Mother Mary comes to me
Speaking words of wisdom, let it be [Ref]

---

4   et It Be lyrics © Sony/ATV Music Publishing LLC

In television interviews Paul denied explicitly this song was religious, and he claimed it was rather a criticism on addicting oneself to hallucinating drugs. He also mentioned that he did not mind if people interpreted the lyrics religiously.

Upon reading these lyrics, *Paul's professed interpretation makes no sense at all*: where is the allusion to drugs, to addiction, or to drug consumption? I do not wish to speculate about his inner motives to deny the obviously religious character of this song. Indeed, religious it is, all invocations of "Mother Mary" referring to the Virgin Mother of God (Paul's parents were of Irish descent), instead of to his own mother Mary. There are at least three important reasons to prove it.

First, the litany of Loreto[5] contains the invocation "Sedes Sapientiae" (Throne of Wisdom). Whence his

---

5 A (Marian) litany is a defined series of Marian invocations. In these invocations, Mary is honored as being Mother of God, whence begotten from here parents without the human ordinary condition of original sin. The faithful do not *adore* her like God wants to be uniquely adored: they only invoke Mary's "supplicating all-might" in order that she intercede for us, sinful humans, by supplicating for mercy at the feet of her divine Son. That Jesus never denies his mother's supplication is dogmatically defined faith. The litany of Loreto was introduced by Pope Paul V in 1571 by a *motu proprio* (a document written by the Pope on his personal initiative). The author of the Wikipedia page on the litany is quite confused when writing that Mary's title *Auxilium Christianorum* (Savior of Christianity) "cannot refer to the battle of Lepanto, as the latter occurred a few months after the promulgation of Paul's *motu proprio*." The Wikipedia author apparently ignores crucial information concerning the naval battle of

mother does not speak words of tender love, like an average mum would do, but she speaks "words of wisdom", which is somehow the prerogative of the Virgin Mary.

Second, according to Paul McCartney himself, his mother coming to him, as in that dream, occurred only once in his life. The lyrics plainly contradict that. They assert that Mary comes whenever he finds himself in times of trouble or darkness. For non-Catholics, it might be useful to add that devout Catholics pray a Loreto-litany daily, being part of the Holy Rosary.

Third, without disruption of continuity, the lyrics mention Mary's answer "to broken-hearted people living in the world agree: for though they may be parted, there is still a chance that they will see." Is his mother so powerful that she can achieve this grace for the world agree? I Don't think so. What I know for sure, on the other

---

Lepanto. As far as the poorly informed Wiki-author is concerned: Toward the end of the 16th century, the naval battle of Lepanto was an inevitable confrontation between Christianity and Islam. Not only Christianity, but also Islam feared the outcome of the clash, although on paper Islam had a marked superiority of vessels. **Since when would it be impossible for a Pope to ask prayers for the outcome of a future event? That is, any event which, due to its political or religious context, will inevitably occur on short term?** Unthinkable for the short-sighted Wiki-author. After the additions made by Pope John Paul II the litany of Loreto was converted into a series of triplets: after an introductory triplet, she is invoked as Mother in three triplets, as Virgin in two, mixed in one, as a Vessel in one, mixed and as a Queen in the final eight triplets.

hand, is that any pretention of his mother regarding such a lofty goal never reached the public dominion.

Fourth, the lyrics literally claim that "when the night is cloudy there is still a light that shines on me, shine until tomorrow, let it be". That is to say, a light shines on him the whole night, every time his life happens to be cloudy. Cloudiness is rule rather than exception in England. Is his mother the nocturnal shining light? Or should we better stick to the Virgin Mary, whom two millennia of Catholic tradition consider as the moon?[6]

Sorry to contradict your own testimony,[7] Paul, but in *Let it be* your lyrics are about the Virgin Mary, and not about your mother, even though she might have been

---

[6] The Virgin Mary being compared to the moon, only holds, theologically speaking, in the sense that she fully reflects all the light projected onto her by the sun (image of God the Son). However, in the famous (because miraculous and miracle-inducing) picture of the Virgin Mary of Guadalupe (Mexico), on Juan Diego's poncho, the Virgin Mary is represented as standing on top of the moon, that is, she is a being far superior than an atmosphere-less, stony conglomerate, circling around our planet. The image came about in a split of a second on the front side of his poncho, during the act of rolling out all his collected flowers to his bishop. According to the tradition of the Church, Juan Diego asked to be received by the bishop after a mystical conversation with a Lady, in his native (Aztec) *Nahuatl* language. That Lady identified herself as the Virgin Mary, "mother of the very true deity", as revered by the newly introduced Spanish religion. She asked him to tell the Church authorities to build a chapel on the place of her appearance to Juan Diego.

[7] I apologize to the reader for directing myself directly to sir Paul McCartney in this paragraph

instrumental in having the Virgin Mary help you in a special way, given the fact that you lost your mother in your tender youth.

You once publicly opened your heart, revealing your tender youth thoughts: you did not fully realize that your mother's death meant you would never see her again on earth. Rather, you were totally upset because of your father's crying. You had never seen *that* happening before. It made you conclude that something had to be extremely wrong, though you did not realize exactly what that was.

This limited understanding of reality is intrinsic to childhood itself, and it makes your remembrance very realistic. Hopefully for you Paul, your denial of the Virgin Mary is Petrine[8] (that is, due to momentary cowardice), and not premeditated (like Judas' kiss).

As far as your song is concerned, its lyrics form a superb prayer, and its melody is unique and exquisite in its simplicity.

John used to poke fun at your melodies, which he considered too simplistic and childish. He may have been

---

8   Peter, the leader of Christ's twelve Apostles, denied the Christ on the evening prior to his execution. In contrast to Judas, he wept over his sin. After his resurrection, Christ made him the first Pope. Knowing the weakness of mankind, he told his first Pope explicitly: "after having repented from however low you might fall, help your brethren to convert, too." Thinking of the Pope as infallible in this sense, is the very opposite of the doctrine of the Catholic Church. That is why there is no sin at all in praying for the conversion of Pope Francis to Catholicism.

right in some cases, like *Octopus's garden*, but his sarcasm was totally misplaced in the case of *Let it be*.[9]

Paul in full Denial Syndrome

---

[9] John could not help it, poor boy, due to his complete lack of a supernatural antenna. There do exist differences between a human without supernatural notion, and an animal, I hope. And if so, what exactly *are* those differences?

CHAPTER 3
Mick Jagger

The Rolling Stones' song writers Keith Richards and Mick Jagger are our next musical geniuses. The lyrics I choose in their case are those of "Angie". It is but a stupid myth that Bob Dylan had such an enormous influence on the Rolling Stones, the Beatles, the Who, and so many other pop groups. Keith Richards is a genuinely creative musician, not at all a plagiarizer, and totally different from Bob Dylan. What the Rolling Stones do have, however, is a legendary but dementing solo guitarist: the permanently stoned Keith Richards. A real tribute to his band name!

The tune and its rendering are spectacular. For example, *Angie* is much "looser" from the un-syncopated[10] or regular metric then their older *Satisfaction:* in the latter song, only the voice is "off-beat" or, in more technical slang, "syncopated". The genius of Mick Jagger is apparent from his very early use, in rock music, of syncopated singing, like in *Satisfaction*: the beat of the four words "I can't get no", just like the four syllables "sa-tis-fac-tion" fall on the second, third-up, first, and third-down beats, respectively. Moreover, the

---

10   https://en.wikipedia.org/wiki/Syncopation

final "no-o" and "tio-on" are duplicated one beat later, that is, on the fourth-down beat, thereby introducing two other syncopations. The Stones' syncopation sounded really spectacular and unique in their time, as their rival innovators and co-nationals, the Beatles, did not use it so pronouncedly.

Mick Jagger was well aware of his own genius. The first time he performed on British television, he started his song halfway the anchorman's introduction, leaving the latter startled, to say the least. Because I merely suspect Keith Richards to be the lyrics writer, I will use his name as standing for the duo. So what is Keith telling us, in *Angie*?

Superficially spoken, he describes a pair of youngsters, having lived together for some time, with the boy expressing his wish to end the relationship because of lack of "satisfaction", a quite principal theme in the Stones. Unlike their earlier song, which does not transcend the level of male sexual potency, *Angie* puts the blame of the near-ended relationship on the lack of money.

Both these "reasons" are a sign of times. They are strictly different from "love": as different as "love" is from "money" and "sexual potency". Unless one would dare to say that rich people love each other more than poor people, or that love between elderly people suddenly stops when mister becomes impotent.

Mick Jagger (Rolling Stones)

Angie (The Rolling Stones)
Richards and Jagger[11]

Angie, when will those clouds all disappear?
Angie, Angie, where will it lead us from here?
With no loving in our souls,
and no money in our coats,
you can't say we're satisfied.
Angie, Angie, you can't say we never tried.
Angie, you're beautiful,
but ain't it time we said good-bye?
Angie, I still love you,
remember all those nights we cried?
All the dreams we held so close,
seemed to all go up in smoke,
let me whisper in your ear:
Angie, Angie, where will it lead us from here?
Oh, Angie, don't you weep,
all your kisses still taste sweet,
I hate that sadness in your eyes.
But Angie, Angie, ain't it time we said good-bye?

---

11 (I Can't Get No) Satisfaction lyrics © Abkco Music, Inc

The next question concerns the use of the word "love". Why does Keith say "I still love you" in *Angie*, while love is the *exclusive reason* for a relation to hold? The only thing I can think of, is that Keith is heavily confused, and the large majority of society with him. That part of society *really believes* that money and sexual orgasm are the founding pillars of happiness, and are impotent of conceiving that "love" has nothing to do with either of them.[12]

Sexually impotent as they may be, they **love** *playing music, in the true sense of the verb. B.B. King and Tracy Chapman sung exactly the same, though more politely.*[13]

---

12 "making love" is a typical stupid invention of the 1960's
13 *The Thrill Is Gone,* Songwriters: Lew Brown and Ray Henderson, © Warner/Chappell Music, Inc.

Chapter 4
Paul Simon

Paul Simon has the unique double talent to write both new tunes, and lyrics at level of poetry.

The lyrics speak in many images about a man's love for his distant lady. His non-responded love ruins the man to such a degree that he loses his faith, and reduces the whole sense of his life to disappearing like rain into the mud for his beloved, even though she is not even aware of it.

Even though these lyrics are infinitely superior to Jagger's, they nonetheless reflect the sign of our times. Losing one's faith due to losing one's beloved is a clear indication of never having had faith in the first place. Or is faith only meant to enjoy a religious gathering because of its social context? We will meet the same theme with REM's "losing my religion".

Enjoy these lyrics of Paul Simon: [14]

---

[14] Kathy's Song lyrics © Universal Music Publishing Group

Kathy's Song
Paul Simon

I hear the drizzle of the rain
Like a memory it falls
Soft and warm continuing
Tapping on my roof and walls
And from the shelter of my mind
Through the window of my eyes
I gaze beyond the rain-drenched streets
To England where my heart lies
My mind's distracted and diffused
My thoughts are many miles away
They lie with you when you're asleep
And kiss you when you start your day
And as a song I was writing is left undone
I don't know why I spend my time
Writing songs I can't believe
With words that tear and strain to rhyme
And so you see I have come to doubt
All that I once held as true
I stand alone without beliefs
The only truth I know is you
And as I watch the drops of rain
Weave their weary paths and die
I know that I am like the rain
There but for the grace of you go I

So, having described the naturally-happy people's fake faith, it is now time to describe those people's fake faith when their natural happiness is taken away from them. Since faith is an exclusively supernatural[15] virtue, the fake faith is nothing but a natural feeling. Although there exist mixed natural and supernatural feelings, fake faith is like feeling hungry before the meal, and feeling satisfied after the meal.

Does one lose the concept that 2+2 make 4, when one loses one's beloved? Do the laws of biology, chemistry, and physics change? So why would *true* faith change, given that *true* faith has nothing whatsoever to do with feelings?[16] Scientific laws exist in much the same way: they are nothing but our partial understanding of God's word which is the universe.

That is the sign of our times: the supernatural impotence of growing in faith, because of a completely disturbed natural understanding of the natural grounds for having faith.

---

15   Natural is everything that is due to natural laws: like physical, chemical, mathematical, and pharmacological laws. Supernatural is everything that belongs to the domain of spirit, which totally transcends the natural level. The supernatural can exist without the natural, but not the other way around.

16   St. Theresa of Ávila always taught her novices never to seek for comfort, consolation, or the supernatural in their prayer, as are extasis, elevations, and the like.

Chapter 4

Paul Simon, always in search of true faith, true love, and above all, true musical beauty

CHAPTER 5
Benny and Björn

As you might know, all ABBA songs are written by Benny Anderson and Björn Ulvaeus, the two super-talents and excellent friends who considered making money more important than taking care of their wives. Their lyrics always convey a deeper message, without however reaching any significant cultural level, nor poetry (although they rhyme). As usual, the two girls sing the songs, Agnetha Fältskog (Björn's ex-wife) the soprano, and Anni-Frid Lyngstad (Benny's ex-wife) the alt. Enjoy the following lyrics:

Clearly, these lyrics are written by men, and very traditional-minded at that (in the sense of anti-feminine). They describe how a less pretty single lady, looking for a friend "when the pretty birds have flown", humiliates herself in all possible ways. Apart from admitting she is not as pretty as those "pretty birds", she keeps offering herself even after a some negatives; third, she promises to do her very best (of course in the sexual sense); fourth, she allows the gentleman to "put her to the test", which implies his being free of "love affairs" (meaning an adult's compromise), in case his first sexual experience with her is not as ecstatic as he imagined.

Take a Chance on Me (ABBA)
Andersson and Ulvaeus[17]

If you change your mind, I'm the first in line
Honey I'm still free, Take a chance on me
If you need me, let me know, gonna be around
If you've got no place to go,
if you're feeling down
If you're all alone
when the pretty birds have flown
Honey I'm still free, take a chance on me
Gonna do my very best and it ain't no lie
If you put me to the test, if you let me try
We can go dancing, we can go walking,
as long as we're together
Listen to some music, maybe just talking,
get to know you better
'Cause you know I've got
So much that I wanna do,
when I dream I'm alone with you, it's magic
You want me to leave it there
afraid of a love affair
But I think you know, that I can't let go

---

[17] Take a Chance on Me lyrics © Universal Music Publishing Group, BMG Rights Management

Benny and Björn (ABBA)

The only sane propositions come later: listening to music, walking, and talking. But, in the end, she confesses she "can't let go", and returns to her previous stupidities: "if you change your mind, I'm the first in line".

What can we read here? A sign of times? I think so. I think what the two BB-boys convey is what the large majority of men think about women: that they are after men, and not *vice versa*. If this is the result of half a century of feminist activism, the latter has failed grossly. A more correct but less kind formulation is that *feminism has actively pushed the humiliation of women* by concentrating their fight on top-directives, instead of what the majority of women presently are: housewives and lower ranked employees. Note that these female *free choices* are the more accentuated, the richer the country.

Nice example: A&A have no problem at all with singing B&B macho texts. They were more interested in getting a bit of human warmth from their husbands. The latter were too nerdish to capture female SOS signals, but enough of sellers to write a song carrying that very title.

Chapter 5

The two super nerds and their loveliest ex-wives shown in BAAB order

Chapter 6
Sting

Sting (born Steve Borden) wrote the song in 1982, after exchanging his wife Frances Tomelty for her best friend, Trudie Styler. In order to avoid being confronted with the enormous wave of negative publicity, Sting retreated to the Caribbean. There he wrote his masterpiece.

Sting comments on his own song:

> I woke up in the middle of the night with that line in my head, sat down at the piano and had written it in half an hour. The tune itself is generic, an aggregate of hundreds of others, but the words are interesting. It sounds like a comforting love song. I didn't realize at the time how sinister it is. I think I was thinking of Big Brother, surveillance and control."

Indeed, Sting says the truth. The lyrics are not at all words of love, but rather a sociopath's or stalker's thoughts. They are a typical expression of a depressive man. That is quite simple to understand, as he had just done a terrible thing: leaving his wife for her best friend. It was but a question of time, and Sting would overcome this period of anxiety, and return to writing normal lyrics. Enjoy the lyrics:

Every Breath You Take
(Sting)
Borden and Summers[18]

Every breath you take, every move you make
Every bond you break, every step you take
I'll be watching you
Every single day, every word you say
Every game you play, every night you stay
I'll be watching you
O can't you see? You belong to me
How my poor heart aches
with every step you take
Every move you make, every vow you break
Every smile you fake, every claim you stake
I'll be watching you
Since you've gone I been lost without a trace
I dream at night I can only see your face
I look around but it's you I can't replace
I keep crying baby please

---

[18] Every Breath You Take lyrics © Sony/ATV Music Publishing LLC

In Sting's experience one sees the direct connection between one's deeds and one's conscience. Every good deed elevates one's conscience, leading supernatural happiness. Every wrong deed depresses one's conscience, leading to a loss of supernatural happiness. The difference between natural and supernatural happiness is the former is associated with strong but momentous feelings (after having eaten one's fill, when taking a shower after jogging, while listening to one's favorite music, and the already mentioned orgasm), while the latter with a very week but permanent consciousness of being a child of God.

The sign of times, implicit in Sting's song, is associated with the natural anxiety of losing his new friend, the wish of somehow controlling the her free choices, and the total ignorance of a supernatural world. This is a clear sign of degeneration, as the first two are incompatible. Even the most convinced agnostic or atheist know that one can impossibly love a computer, however human its behavior and exterior appearance. What a man does when visiting a whore, has nothing to do with love. It is nothing but assisted masturbation. This is exactly what a computer can give a lonely man: assistance in a purely selfish act. On the other hand, supernatural love is the opposite: it consists in continually searching opportunities to please one's beloved, even when the necessary deeds require a sacrifice,[19] yes, heroic if needed. The moments of "making

---

[19] This word reminds one of three other musical geniuses: Michael Stipes, Bryan Adams, and Elton John.

love" will come spontaneously, even when not as often as mister genius wishes.

*A genius: musically highly gifted,
yet socially poorly adapted*

Chapter 7
Bono

The music of "Where the Streets Have No Name" is due to guitarist The Edge, and the lyrics to Bono (born Paul David Hewson). The lyrics were inspired by a story that Bono heard about Belfast, Northern Ireland, where a person's religion and income were evident by the street on which they lived.[20] He contrasted this with the anonymity he felt when visiting Ethiopia, saying:

> The guy in the song recognizes this contrast and thinks about a world where there aren't such divisions, a place where the streets have no name. To me, that's the way a great rock 'n' roll concert should be: a place where everyone comes together... Maybe that's the dream of all art: to break down the barriers and the divisions between people and touch upon the things that matter the most to us all.

The video was directed by Meiert Avis and produced by Michael Hamlyn and Ben Dossett. The band attracted

---

20 Wikipedia, https://en.wikipedia.org/wiki/Where_the_Streets_Have_No_Name

over 1,000 people during the video's filming, which took place on the rooftop of a liquor store in Downtown Los Angeles (on the roof of a liquor store at the corner of 7th St. and S. Main St.) on 27 March 1987. The band's performance on a rooftop in a public place was a reference to The Beatles' final concert, as depicted in the film *Let It Be*. The video won the Grammy Award for Best Performance Music Video at the 1989 Grammy Awards.

Bono, who compared many of his lyrics prior to The Joshua Tree to sketches, said that

> "*Where the Streets Have No Name* is more like the U2 of old than any of the other songs on the LP,[21] because it's a sketch — I was just trying to sketch a location, maybe a spiritual location, maybe a romantic location. I was trying to sketch a feeling."

Bono has expressed mixed opinions about the open-ended lyrics:

> "I can look at it now and recognize that [the song] has one of the most banal couplets in the history of pop music. But it also contains some of the biggest ideas. In a curious way, that seems to work. If you get any way heavy about these things, you don't communicate. But if you're flip or throwaway about it, then you do. That's one of

---

21   Joshua Tree

the paradoxes I've come to terms with."

According to Bono,

> "the song is ostensibly about transcendence, elevation, whatever you want to call it"

In the last paragraph, Bono teaches us a good lesson of how to popularize new ideas. I have to admit I didn't know about it, but it sounds like good advice. Just above that paragraph, Bono claims that his song is ostensibly about transcendence, and a "sketch of a spiritual location".

Bono does not feel ashamed to pose with an old man: History will confirm that this old man was none less than Saint John Paul the Great

Where the Streets Have no Name (U2)
Clayton, Evans, Mullen, Hewson[22]

I want to run, I want to hide
I want to tear down the walls
that hold me inside
I wanna reach out and touch the flame
Where the streets have no name
I want to feel sunlight on my face
I see that dust cloud disappear without a trace
I wanna take shelter from the poison rain
Where the streets have no name
We're still building then burning down love
Burning down love
And when I go there, I go there with you
It's all I can do
The city's a flood and our love turns to rust
We're beaten and blown by the wind
Trampled into dust
I'll show you a place high on the desert plain
Where the streets have no name

---

[22] Where the Streets Have No Name lyrics © Universal Music Publishing Group

Chapter 8
Roger Waters

As far as I know, Roger Waters wrote both the lyrics and music for "another brick in the wall". His composer's qualities and his artistic performance are equally excellent. Waters used to play the bass. At Tokyo International Forum on March 30, 2002, in the guitar solo towards after the choir of "another brick in the wall", halfway he takes over the guitar solo from David Gilmour. The loss of his voice was probably the best thing that could have happened to Waters: he suddenly plays an amazing staccato that lifts his guitar solo to unknown heights.

The foremost problem for teachers in western (non-)cultures is the often complete lack of parental interest. Those parents think their role is only to threaten the teacher when their kid underperforms. I believe American law is much too soft on those parents. Their behavior is a direct indication of their not being suited as educators of their own children, and of their need of serious help. It is not the teachers, but the rotten marriages that are "just another brick in the wall".

Roger Waters is no doubt an amazing musical talent. However, his societal views are somewhat limited, to put it kindly. Typical of moral liberalism, or libertarianism if you wish.

Another Brick in the Wall
(Pink Floyd)
Roger Waters[23]

We don't need no education
We don't need no thought control
No dark sarcasm in the classroom
Teachers leave them kids alone
Hey, teachers, leave them kids alone
All in all you're just another brick in the wall
We don't need no education
We don't need no thought control
No dark sarcasm in the classroom
Teachers leave those kids alone
Hey teachers, leave those kids alone
All in all you're just another brick in the wall
"Wrong, do it again! Wrong, do it again!"
"If you don't eat yer meat,
you can't have any pudding
How can you have any pudding
if you don't eat yer meat?"
"You, yes, you behind the bike sheds,
stand still, laddy"

---

23 Another Brick in the Wall (Part 2) lyrics © BMG Rights Management

Fast to criticize others, and slow to introspect: only the latter walk of life allows one to change positively, searching to make life more agreeable to others. Waters is a typical egotistical child of his time. Take his "Mother" lyrics, for example. Every mother who bore and gave birth to an own child has an exclusive, mysterious bond with her child – a bond that gracious Roger knows no better than to make fun of. How vomitingly cheap.

Obviously, many mothers tend to be a little possessive with regard to their children. So what? Is Waters not enough of a man to tell his mother in a loving way that she goes too far at some point? Alas, he lacks the very balls to do so. He does, however, have the balls to put all blame on *her*. *She* built too high a wall around her baby, and due to *her*, he refused the one girl of his life.[24]

---

[24] Dear Roger, who gave you the right to inform the general public about your mother's shortcomings? If you really want to sing about shortcomings, then be a man, and confess your own! You might draw profitably from St. Augustine.

Mother (Pink Floyd)
Roger Waters

Mother do you think they'll drop the bomb?
Mother do you think they'll like this song?
Mother do you think they'll try to break my balls?
Mother should I build the wall?
Mother should I run for President?
Mother should I trust the government?
Mother will they put me in the firing mine?
Is it just a waste of time?
Hush now baby, baby, don't you cry
Mama's gonna make all your nightmares come true
Mama's gonna put all her fears into you
Mama's gonna keep you right here under her wing
She won't let you fly, but she might let you sing
Mama's gonna keep baby cozy and warm
Ooh baby, of course mama's gonna help build the wall
Mother do you think she's good enough for me?
Mother do you think she's dangerous to me?
Mother will she tear your little boy apart?
Mother will she break my heart?
(...) Mother, did it need to be so high?

Roger Waters (Pink Floyd)

Deeply frustrated, spoiled and fatherless child

The negative figure legend represents my own impression of Roger Waters. Please do not take it as pointing out his weaknesses. Put someone in an American prison, however harmless and kind, and that person will leave that prison as an animal. Therefore, one says nothing but the truth when describing that person like a brute. However, no judgement is implied whatsoever, because nobody knows where that brutality came from. It makes quite a difference if one has obtained an excellent education of two loving parents, or one did not. When Waters puts all the blame of the wall on his mother, this does not logically imply that it is his fault that he acts like a child. However, the historical fact remains that he did act like a child. This is his character: He always blames the world outside, and is utterly unable to introspect and find some tiny flaw in his own decisions or actuations.

The last sentence of his song

Mother, did it need to be so high?

summarizes his griefs toward her. *She* built the wall. *She* built it so high that he was unable to reach out to his girlfriend. *She* made him completely dependent on her. *He* was not to blame, *he* did everything well in his life. This reminds me of the Frenchman Sartre: "L'enfer, c'est les autres"; translated: "hell, that's the others".

Well, I must admit Sartre, who never declared anything worth reading, that from the concept of hell he understood at least a little. Hell is indeed the others, although not *all others.* Hell is only *all others in hell,* plus the primary concept: One having freely and firmly chosen to be where God is not.

Chapter 9
Freddy Mercury

Freddy's masterpiece, *Bohemian Rhapsody*, is so autobiographical that he asked his band (Queen) to play that feature down in interviews, and not insist on inquiring for its meaning. My posthumous interpretation is that the murder he confesses to his mother is his own "suicide". That suicide is not meant in a literal sense, but in a spiritual one: it marks the day he freely and consciously decided to give free rein to his homosexual preference, possibly after years of inner fights to follow his conscience. This could explain the word "confession". The fact that he confesses his sin to his mother is a sign of two coinciding facts: first, his deep love for his mother, and second, his realization that his mother would disapprove of his choice — independently of her still being alive or not.

I admire Freddy a lot, as a person, and as an artist. The *Bohemian Rhapsody* is, from the merely musical point of view, very "daring" because of its double length as compared to the average pop song, its mixture of hard rock with elements of classical music, and its precious transitions from one genre to another one; all this, without losing its inner unity.

Bohemian Rhapsody (Queen)
Freddie Mercury[25]

Is this the real life? Is this just fantasy?
Caught in a landslide, no escape from reality
Open your eyes. look up to the skies and see
I'm just a poor boy, I need no sympathy
Because I'm easy come, easy go
A little high, little low
Anyway the wind blows, doesn't really matter to me
Mama, just killed a man
Put a gun against his head
Pulled my trigger, now he's dead
Mama, life had just begun
But now I've gone and thrown it all away
Mama, oh oh
Didn't mean to make you cry
If I'm not back again this time tomorrow
Carry on, carry on, as if nothing really matters
Too late, my time has come
Sends shivers down my spine
Body's aching all the time
Goodbye everybody I've got to go
Gotta leave you all behind and face the truth
Mama, oh oh (anyway the wind blows)

---

[25] Bohemian Rhapsody lyrics © Sony/ATV Music Publishing LLC

Freddy Mercury

I see a little silhouetto of a man
Scaramouch, Scaramouch will you do the Fandango
Thunderbolt and lightning very very frightening me
Gallileo, Gallileo, Gallileo, Gallileo, figaro, magnifico
I'm just a poor boy and nobody loves me
He's just a poor boy from a poor family
Spare him his life from this monstrosity
Easy come easy go will you let me go
Bismillah, no we will not let you go, let him go
Bismillah, we will not let you go, let him go
Bismillah, we will not let you go, let me go
(Will not let you go) let me go (never, never let you go) let me go (never let me go)
Oh oh no, no, no, no, no, no, no
Oh mama mia, mama mia, mama mia let me go
Beelzebub has a devil put aside for me for me for me
So you think you can stop me and spit in my eye
So you think you can love me and leave me to die
Oh baby can't do this to me baby
Just gotta get out just gotta get right outta here
Oh oh oh yeah, oh oh yeah
Nothing really matters, anyone can see
Nothing really matters, nothing really matters to me
Anyway the wind blows

The song starts out with the typical "substance user" kind of question: whether he perceives real life or a fantasy. The landslide shaking him around is so strong and impossible to influence by his thoughts, that he finally concludes that his perceptions are indeed due to real life, which offers "no escape": reality is one, and neither allows for "transformations to other lives", nor for reincarnation in general. According to Wikipedia,[26] reincarnation is a central tenet of many Indian religions (like Jainism, Buddhism, Sikhism and Hinduism[27]). Great ancient Greeks, like Pythagoras, Socrates, and Plato, believed in reincarnation, too. It is also a common belief of various ancient and modern religions such as Spiritism, Theosophy, and Eckankar, and as an esoteric belief in many streams of Orthodox Judaism. It is found as well in some tribal societies around the world, in places such as Australia and South America.

To date, not the remotest indication for reincarnation exists, as far as I know. No such thing as reincarnation for Freddy either, whose parents educated their son in their Zoroastrian[28] faith. "Open your eyes, look up to the skies

---

26   https://en.wikipedia.org/wiki/Reincarnation
27   there exist Hindu beliefs which only accept an afterlife, like Christianity
28   Excerpt from Wikipedia: "Zoroastrianism, or Mazdayasna, is one of the world's oldest religions that remains active. It is a monotheistic faith (i.e. a single creator god), centered in a dualistic cosmology of good and evil and an eschatology predicting the ultimate destruction of evil. Ascribed to the teachings of the Iranian-speaking prophet Zoroaster (also known as Zarathustra), it exalts a deity of wisdom, Ahura Mazda (Wise Lord), as its Supreme Being. With possible roots

and see" is Freddy's prayer to God. He confesses his humility and reacts to God like Peter in his first encounter, just after the miraculous fish capture: "go away from me, Lord, because I am a sinner". In Freddy's words: "I'm just a poor boy, I need no sympathy; because I'm easy come, easy go, little high, little low".

He confesses having sent God out of his soul: "Anyway the wind blows, doesn't really matter to me, to me". His confession to "Mama" continues: "life had just begun", possibly a reference to Queen's worldwide success. Knowing that his choice deeply hurts his mother's feelings, he sings he "didn't mean to make [her] cry". If he does not repent during the night ("if I'm not back again this time tomorrow") he advises his mother to "Carry on, carry on, as if nothing really matters", because for himself it will already be "too late, my time has come". The "shivers down my spine, body's aching all the time" prophesizes the pains he will be suffering in Zoroastrian Afterlife. His death drawing nearer, he takes his leave: "goodbye everybody I've got to go; gotta leave you all behind and face the truth". The latter might be a reference to his divine Judgement.

> dating back to the second millennium BC, Zoroastrianism enters recorded history in the 5th century BC. Along with a Mithraic Median prototype and a Zurvanist Sassanid successor, it served as the state religion of the pre-Islamic Iranian empires for more than a millennium, from around 600 BC to AD 650. Zoroastrianism was suppressed from the 7th century onwards following the Muslim conquest of Persia of 633–654. Recent estimates place the current number of Zoroastrians at around 190,000, with most living in India and in Iran."

I am convinced that Freddy's half-life-long fight against his pedophilic tendencies is very important in God's eyes, as are his feelings of deep regret when having acted upon them, and his consequent urgent wish to confess. This is what I, as biased as anyone else, see in his suffering eyes.

After "I know..." Freddy contemplates himself in the court of divine Justice, as if his spirit were uncoupled from his body ("the silhouette of a little man"). Not yet knowing how God's Justice will turn out for him, he describes the initial court procedures as a fight between an Archangel (Bismillah, or "In the name of God" in Arabic) and Beelzebub (one of the many Jewish names for the devil), who both claim his soul.

Scaramouche is the French name of an Italian clown "Scaramuccio", meaning "skirmisher". The clown ridiculed the cowardice of Spanish hidalgo's (nobility) in battle, as compared to Italian mercenaries. In Freddy's song, Scaramouche stands for lower angels, subject to the devil. The "fandango" is a typical south-Spanish dance, usually in triple meter (i.e., like a waltz). It is traditionally accompanied by guitars, castanets, and Andalusian hand-clapping.[29] Galileo refers to heaven, and all other o-ended words (fandango, figaro, magnifico) are mere rhymers. In short, Freddy views a divine trial, in which he opens the court proceedings by asking, ironically, that a fallen angel

---

29 In Andalusian hand-clapping, at the end of a couplet, part of the hand-clappers change from on-beat to off-beat clapping, yielding the quite stupefying effect of double-frequency hand-clapping

dance for him. This request betrays that Freddy himself has no hope on a positive divine judgement.[30]

*Freddy Mercury, the lyric defender of the supernatural,
not as a mere abstract principle
but as a Living Being and Creator of man,
Who gave man the funny freedom
to offend his own Creator*

---

30 That is most reasonable since there is no Christ neither virgin Mary in Zoroastrianism.

Chapter 9

*Scaramouche, who obtained the Creator's permission
to tease Freddie for a little while
just like He did with Job of old*

CHAPTER 10
Mark Knopfler

Knopfler's band is called "Dire Straits", because Mark loves describing hopeless misery. He hardly smiles when he performs. The obvious reason is that he must always be quite concentrated on alternating his voice with response-like guitar solos. In my view, he is the top 1 musician of his century in the art of corresponding his whispered lines with guitar lines. There are plenty of rockers playing faster than he does, more virtuous than he does, but they do not even come close to him: their virtuosity is hollow, repetitive, devoid of meaning and emotion, as compared to Knopfler. When Knopfler plays a song about the sun, one can see the latter rising from his guitar, so to speak. Mark's best song is Telegraph Road, and its lyrics are not scarce in real dire straits: depression, misery, and poverty.

The first part of this song ends with the words "like a rolling river": it describes how a commercially rich mining town grew out of nothing, due to an unnamed, lonely pioneer, who came walking with a sack on his back, and started to dig for ore.

The second part changes abruptly from perspective: instead of viewing facts thorough historians' spectacles, the rest of the song lyrics are written in first person. They describe how the miner's town's rise to wealth and decay to debris affect his relation with his beloved. Once she used to love and caress him, but now she "acts a little colder, like she don't seem to care". However, Mark believes in her, and promises her to take her away from the ruined town.

The only thing we know about the town is that it was rather a metropole, containing twice-six-lane avenues with "rivers of headlights". Detroit might be a guess, although that is not Mark's key point. His main messages are:

- all people have a fundamental right to earn a dignified living;
- whenever people earn less, their relations become more stressed.

These two messages are quite important. Knopfler succeeded in combining excellent music with lyrics of a high cultural level, and beautiful imagery.

Telegraph Road
(Dire Straits)
Mark Knopfler[31]

A long time ago came a man on a track
Walking thirty miles with a sack on his back
And he put down his load
where he thought it was the best
Made a home in the wilderness
He built a cabin and a winter store
And he ploughed up the ground by the cold lake shore
And the other travelers came walking down the track
And they never went further, no,
they never went back
Then came the churches, then came the schools
Then came the lawyers, then came the rules
Then came the trains and the trucks with their load
And the dirty old track was the Telegraph Road
Then came the mines, then came the ore
Then there was the hard times, then there was a war
Telegraph sang a song about the world outside
Telegraph Road got so deep and so wide
Like a rolling river
And my radio says tonight it's gonna freeze
People driving home from the factories
There's six lanes of traffic, three lanes moving slow
I used to like to go to work but they shut it down

---

[31] Telegraph Road lyrics © Universal Music Publishing Group

I've got a right to go to work
but there's no work here to be found
and they say we're gonna have to pay what's owed
We're gonna have to reap
from some seed that's been sowed
And the birds up on the wires and the telegraph poles
They can always fly away from this rain and this cold
You can hear them singing out their telegraph code
All the way down the Telegraph Road
Well, I'd sooner forget, but I remember those nights
Yeah, life was just a bet on a race between the lights
You had your hand on my shoulder,
you had your hand in my hair
Now you act a little colder like you don't seem to care
But just believe in me baby and I'll take you away
From out of this darkness and into the day
From these rivers of headlights, these rivers of rain
From the anger that lives
on the streets with these names
'Cause I've run every red light on memory lane
I've seen desperation explode into flames
And I don't wanna see it again
From all of these signs saying
"sorry but we're closed"
All the way down the Telegraph Road

Mark Knopfler

Mark Knopfler: a true King of vocal question and guitar answer[32]

---

[32] When he is not playing solo's, he sings a sentence, ending it with a guitar-played cliffhanger, which takes him to the next sentence: sometimes continuously, sometimes with generous overlap

Chapter 11
Don Henley

The outstanding song "Hotel California", interpreted by the Eagles, clearly speaks of the awfully degrading effects of cannabis or marijuana.[33] A lone and tired visitor approaches a strange hotel that "it could be heaven and it could be hell". After entering the hotel (a figure of taking marijuana for the first time) he discovers, in panic, that there is no possible way out (a figure for the impossibility to stop using marijuana).

The song is structured as three times two couplets with two refrains linking them.

The first couplet sings the moment of personal weakness and self-pity, specifically in the words "my head grew heavy and my sight grew dim, I had to stop for the night". These are all conscience-easing excuses invented by the visitor, in order to appease his conscience before taking marijuana for the first time.

The second couplet presents the big seducer, or the devil herself, in the form of an attractive lady showing the hotel to the visitor.

---

33 In this respect, it is a brother song to Neil Young, who also complains about losing half his band whenever they approach a metropole.

The third couplet describes the devil in more detail: addicted to wealth ("her mind is tiffany[34]-twisted, she got a Mercedes bends"), with many boys dancing for her (those boys impersonate regular users). The "bends" (instead of "Bentz") reinforce the girl's contorted, perverted mind.

The fourth couplet mentions the Captain's words "we haven't had that spirit here since nineteen sixty nine", which probably stands for the year in which EZ began the large-scale introduction of marijuana in the US. "That spirit" is a spirit of the visitor's freedom, which the devil is going to destroy as soon as she can.

The fifth couplet contains the devil's whisper "we are all just prisoners here, of our own device", the latter words referring to the free will of all hotel bookers. It ends with the beautiful image of sniffers who cut the white marijuana into dust: "And in the master's chambers, they gathered for the feast; they stab it with their steely knives, but they just can't kill the beast". The "beast" represents marijuana, which can't be killed, no matter how often one cuts it, as it is already composed of dust. Superior beauty is achieved by don Henley, upon putting heavy emphasis and anti-rhythmic pronunciation on the three consecutive words "just can't kill", while "beast" is co-rhythmic again.

The final couplet has the visitor say: "Last thing I remember". This refers to the fact that the use of marijuana knocked him out to such an extent that, after the night man's refusal to let him leave the hotel, the novel visitor does not remember anything anymore.

---

[34] An expensive jewelry store

Hotel California (Eagles)
Felder, Henley, and Frey[35]

On a dark desert highway, cool wind in my hair
Warm smell of colitas, rising up through the air
Up ahead in the distance, I saw a shimmering light
My head grew heavy and my sight grew dim
I had to stop for the night.
There she stood in the doorway;
I heard the mission bell
And I was thinking to myself
'This could be heaven or this could be Hell'
Then she lit up a candle and she showed me the way
There were voices down the corridor,
I thought I heard them say
Ref: Welcome to the Hotel California
Such a lovely place (such a lovely place)
Such a lovely face.
Plenty of room at the Hotel California
Any time of year (any time of year)
you can find it here
Her mind is Tiffany-twisted,
she got the Mercedes bends
She got a lot of pretty, pretty boys,
that she calls friends
How they dance in the courtyard,

---

[35] Hotel California lyrics © Warner/Chappell Music, Inc, Universal Music Publishing Group

sweet summer sweat
Some dance to remember,
some dance to forget
So I called up the Captain,
'Please bring me my wine'
He said, 'we haven't had that spirit here since
nineteen sixty-nine'
And still those voices are calling from far away,
Wake you up in the middle of the night
Just to hear them say [Ref]
Mirrors on the ceiling,
The pink champagne on ice
And she said, 'we are all just prisoners here,
of our own device'
And in the master's chambers,
They gathered for the feast
They stab it with their steely knives,
But they just can't kill the beast
Last thing I remember, I was
Running for the door
I had to find the passage back
to the place I was before
'Relax' said the night man,
'We are programmed to receive.
You can check out any time you like,
But you can never leave!'

Don Henley

A Masterpiece like Hotel California comes but once in a century, and never by sheer luck
(but always after sweating off one's brow)

CHAPTER 12
Michael Stipe

For Stipe I chose the lyrics of "losing my religion", my most cherished song of R.E.M: an American, alternative-rock band from Athens, Georgia, formed in 1980.

Below I quote some selected Wikipedia passages:[36]

> R.E.M. guitarist Peter Buck wrote the main riff and chorus to the song on a mandolin while watching television one day. Buck had just bought the instrument and was attempting to learn how to play it, recording the music as he practiced. Buck said that "when I listened back to it the next day, there was a bunch of stuff that was really just me learning how to play mandolin, and then there's what became 'Losing My Religion', and then a whole bunch more of me learning to play the mandolin."
>
> In the song, Michael Stipe sings the lines "That's me in the corner/That's me in the spotlight/ Losing my religion". The phrase "losing my religion" is an expression from the southern region of the United States that means losing

---

36 https://en.m.wikipedia.org/wiki/Losing_My_Religion

one's temper or civility, or "being at the end of one's rope." Stipe told The New York Times the song was about romantic expression. He told Q that "Losing My Religion" is about "someone who pines for someone else. It's unrequited love, what have you." Stipe compared the song's theme to "Every Breath You Take" by The Police, saying, "It's just a classic obsession pop song. I've always felt the best kinds of songs are the ones where anybody can listen to it, put themselves in it and say, 'Yeah, that's me'."

Indeed, big music playing houses always want their artists to sing love songs. Hence, Stipes tells them nonsense. If "losing my religion" in his song really means "being at the end of my rope", then what is the southern American slang meaning of "I'm choosing my confessions"?

I think the song is what it says it is: a dream about his trying to keep up with the religious pace of his beloved. He tries very hard but he feels he has not the least idea of supernatural things to even make a first religious step toward his friend. This interpretation makes the first two lines understandable: if life is already bigger than you (a deeply religious woman), how much bigger is life than me (who am not even able to believe in anything supernatural)? You (believer) are not me (unbeliever)![37]

---

[37] The only part not fitting my interpretation is the refrain sentence "I think I thought I saw you try"

Losing My Religion (REM)
Berry, Stipe, Buck, and Mills[38]

Oh, life is bigger
It's bigger than you and you are not me
The lengths that I will go to
The distance in your eyes
Oh no, I've said too much
I set it up
That's me in the corner
That's me in the spotlight
Losing my religion
Trying to keep up with you
And I don't know if I can do it
Oh no, I've said too much
I haven't said enough
I thought that I heard you laughing
I thought that I heard you sing
I think I thought I saw you try
Every whisper
Of every waking hour
I'm choosing my confessions
Trying to keep an eye on you
Like a hurt lost and blinded fool, fool
Oh no, I've said too much

---

38 Losing My Religion lyrics © Warner/Chappell Music, Inc, Universal Music Publishing Group

I set it up
Consider this
The hint of the century
Consider this
The slip that brought me to my knees failed
What if all these fantasies
Come flailing around
Now I've said too much
I thought that I heard you laughing
I thought that I heard you sing
I think I thought I saw you try
But that was just a dream
That was just a dream
That's me in the corner
That's me in the spotlight
Losing my religion
Trying to keep up with you
And I don't know if I can do it
Oh no, I've said too much
I haven't said enough
I thought that I heard you laughing
I thought that I heard you sing
I think I thought I saw you try
But that was just a dream
Try, cry
Why try?
That was just a dream, just a dream, just a dream
Dream

Michael Stipe

I believe this song is not at all about love, although it seems like, in order to fool the publisher. In reality, it is much, much deeper than an ordinary love song. A grateful comparison is always the loser-lyrics of a great artist called Robbie Williams, like in "Feel":

> I just wanna feel real love
> In a life ever after, there's a hole in my soul
> You can see it in my face
> It's a real big place

In sharp contrast, Stipes' rather is an honest autobiographical confession of his impotence to believe in God, even when his own beloved tries to help him do so. Such inability is not within Stipes' natural reach: Nothing wrong here. Before even trying to step up to a supernatural level, one should first get rid, on a mere natural level, of more than a century brainwashing by the media-controlling mafia.

Dreamy Boys Suffering From Rapid Eye Movement

CHAPTER 13
Phil Collins

Some geniuses, like Englishman Phil Collins, are mentally disturbed to such degree to call their whore "Mama", while ejaculating dirty sounds.[39]

Below two close-ups of Phil Collins singing "Mama" with Genesis at Wembly, July 1987.

---

[39] As Collins looks like a psychiatrically normal fellow, to me this songs seems a clear case of having sold one's soul to the devil

Chapter 13

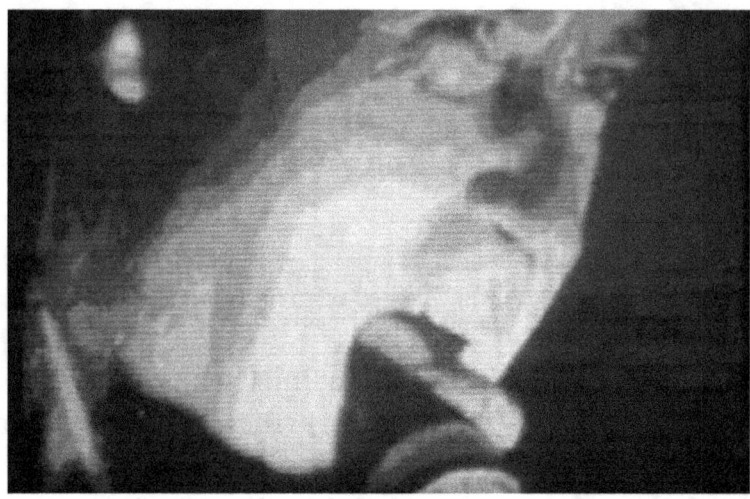

Upon pronouncing the word "argh" he pulls out his tong all over the microphone, licking it with the bottom of his tongue, while the illumination of his face turns yellow. I've never seen the tongue-master himself (Mick Jagger) doing something remotely as filthy as this.

In the following we present the lyrics of one of Collins' many masterpieces: Mama.

Mama (Genesis)
Collins and Smith[40]

I can't see you, Mama
But I can hardly wait
Ooh, to touch and to feel you, Mama
Oh, I just can't keep away

In the heat and the steam of the city
Oh, it's got me running and I just can't brake
So say you'll help me, Mama
'Cause it's getting so hard, oh

Now I can't keep you, Mama
But I know you're always there
You listen, you teach me, Mama
And I know inside you care

So get down, down here beside me
Oh, you ain't going nowhere
No I won't hurt you, Mama
But it's getting so hard, oh

Can't you see me here, Mama?
Mama, Mama, Mama please

---

40 Mama lyrics © BMG Rights Management (UK) Limited, Kassner Associated Publishers Ltd., Df & A Publishing, New York House Music, Fede Yon Music, Picadilly Music Corp., Temple Music (Gb), and Polygram Music Publ Ltd.

Can't you feel my heart?
Can't you feel my heart?
Can't you feel my heart, oh?

Now listen to me, Mama, Mama, Mama
You're taking away my last chance
Don't take it away
Can't you feel my heart?

It's hot, too hot for me, Mama
But I can hardly wait
Oh my eyes they're burning, Mama
And I can feel my body shake

Don't stop, don't stop me, Mama
Oh make the pain, make it go away, hey hey
No, I won't hurt you, Mama
But it's getting so hard

Now I can't see you, Mama
But I know you're always there
You taunt, you tease me, Mama
But I never, never, never can keep away

It's the heat and the steam of the city
Oh, you got me running and I just can't brake
So stay, don't leave me, Mama
'Cause it's getting so hard, oh

Don't go, no no, don't go
Don't go

Phil Collins

Lots of words for a tiny message: "I'm so sex-addicted, that my dick escapes control". Oh yes, he calls his whore "Mama". How sweet.[41]

Born and raised in west London, Collins played drums from the age of five and completed drama school training, which secured him various roles as a child actor. He then pursued a music career, joining Genesis in 1970 as their drummer and becoming lead singer in 1975 following the departure of Peter Gabriel. Collins began a solo career in the 1980s. Collins' masterpiece, in my opinion, is "Against All Odds", although he did not write the song himself (it is from Arif Mardin).

He was unique for his "gated reverb" drum sound. Collins is one of the world's best-selling artists: he is one of only two recording artists, along with Paul McCartney, who have sold over 100 million records worldwide both as solo artists and separately as principal members of a band. He has won all awards and Halls of Fame one can possibly imagine. Given all these huge successes, it is not a real surprise that something went quite wrong with Phil.

His parents might have been too much focused on driving their kid to excellency (in drumming and acting), and not enough on preparing him for the many dangers involved in being a star. In this sense, Phil is the typical product of an ego-centered education. This implies two major educational consequences: First, Phil runs into a tendency of self-conceit. Second, Phil has very few real

---

41   My puke escapes control

friends (of the kind that would help you out of a depression, an addiction, or debt issues), but many fake friends (those who last as long as they can feed on your successes).

These educational mistakes are due to earlier-generation educational mistakes. This is a never ending chain: It does not explain the error itself, but only its transfer from one generation to the next. In the end, it is a societal problem. It might not be so bad an idea to help parents with free education courses: e.g., during expectation, once per month an evening in the city hall.

Anyway, part of this consideration is theoretical, because of Phil's huge talent. According to Barbara Speake, founder of the eponymous stage school Collins later attended, "Phil was always special; aged five he entered a Butlins talent contest singing Davy Crockett, but he stopped the orchestra halfway through to tell them they were in the wrong key."

CHAPTER 14
Eric Clapton

Englishman Eric Clapton so much loved his deceased son, that the wanted him to be in heaven. In this song Eric tells us of his vision of a posthumous meeting with his boy.

The first verse with in-built refrain (together 6 lines) has Eric Clapton asking his son if he still knows his name, and if he would still relate to him as a loving father to a loving son. The refrain is a personal meditation, independently of whether he speaks those words to his son, or overthinks them in his own mind: "I must be strong and carry on, 'cause I know I don't belong here in heaven." It is like as if he were saying thanks to God for offering him the opportunity to greet his son, even though he knows his eternity is not there.

The second verse betrays his strong longing to staying with his son: He asks him to hold his hand and help him stand. The second refrain repeats the same idea as the first one. Then begins the bridge. Therein Eric says: "Time can bring you down, time can bend your knees; time can break your heart, have you begging please". With these words Eric confesses his self-conceit since his tender youth, in which he lived far from God, convinced of not needing Him, even though he felt God was continually whispering for attention in his heart and in his mind. In the refrain, concluding the bridge, he repeats the main refrain idea, this time with some pre-bargaining with God: "beyond the door there's peace I'm sure".

The last verse plus refrain repeat the first one.

Eric's "confession" is a very interesting one. It is a profoundly meant, pious prayer to God, in which he asks forgiveness for all his sins, on the only condition that, although he knows he does not gather the necessary elements of holiness to make it to heaven, he at least be accepted to sit right behind the door. This grants him that, every time the door opens, he might peak inside and see his son's eternal bliss.

Consider the following quote:

> Clapton's second group, formed in 1969, bore the name "Blind Faith". Although it only yielded one LP and one arena-circuit tour, the name of the band is significant, as Clapton was a blind man searching for faith. In the 1970s his international fame continued rising, while Clapton sunk more and more deeply into drug and alcohol addiction. As the band broke up, he found rest in his Surrey residence. There he fought a heroin addiction. In the Concert for Bangladesh in August 1971 he passed out on stage, yet managed to finish his performance after revival. In 1974, Clapton was clean from heroin, although he compensated every step backward in drug addiction to one forward in alcohol. Clapton's philanthropy shone brightest in 1998, when he founded the "Crossroads Centre on Antigua". This was a medical facility for recovering substance abusers. He founded it while still recovering from

Eric Clapton

alcohol and drug addictions himself. On 5 August 1976, Clapton provoked an uproar and lingering controversy when he spoke out against increasing immigration during a concert in Birmingham. Visibly intoxicated, Clapton voiced his support of controversial political candidate Enoch Powell, and announced on stage that Britain was in danger of becoming a "black colony". Among other things, Clapton said, "Keep Britain white!" which was at the time a National Front slogan. In an interview from October 1976 with Sounds magazine, Clapton said that he was not a political person and that his rambling remarks that night were not appropriate. In a 2004 interview with Uncut, Clapton referred to Powell as "outrageously brave". He complained that the UK was "inviting people in as cheap labor and then putting them in ghettos." In 2004, Clapton told an interviewer for Scotland on Sunday, "There's no way I could be a racist. It would make no sense." In his 2007 autobiography, Clapton claimed to be "oblivious to it all." In a December 2007 interview with Melvyn Bragg on The South Bank Show, Clapton told Bragg that he wasn't a racist but still believed Powell's comments were relevant. On 20 March 1991, Clapton's four-year-old son, Conor, fell from the 53rd-floor window of his mother's friend's New York City apartment. Eight days later, Conor's funeral took place in Clapton's home village in Ripley, Surrey. This event finally removed the platelets from his eyes.

I will conclude this chapter with some personal opinions.

First, I do not believe that Eric is a racist: that is too easy a reproach.

Second, I do not see why "keep England white" is a racist claim, when all immigrants happen to be of color. It is nothing but a blunt, somewhat stupid way, to say "stop immigration into England, at least until we've got our white mess under control."

Third, his appraisal of Enoch Powell could very well be limited to the latter's stand on the immigration issue. Voting for a person does not mean agreeing with everything that person claims, or stands for. In politics, one most often votes for the least evil. Those who make out other people for racists (disregarding the most stupid part of our world, which gathers under the name Ku Klux Klan), are frustrates themselves. They are like those shouting "nie wieder" (German for "never again", referred to World War II), but, come the opportunity, would turn out even worse animals than Hitler himself.

Tears In Heaven
Clapton and Jennings[42]

Would you know my name
If I saw you in heaven?
Would it be the same
If I saw you in heaven?
I must be strong and carry on
'Cause I know I don't belong here in heaven
Would you hold my hand
If I saw you in heaven?
Would you help me stand
If I saw you in heaven?
I'll find my way through night and day
'Cause I know I just can't stay here in heaven
Time can bring you down, time can bend your knees
Time can break your heart, have you begging please, begging please
Beyond the door there's peace I'm sure
And I know there'll be no more tears in heaven

---

[42] Tears In Heaven lyrics © Warner/Chappell Music, Inc, Universal Music Publishing Group

Chapter 14

*Eric Clapton, the suffering soul,
who makes billions happy with his beautiful songs*

Chapter 15
Bruce Springsteen

In songs like "Your Home Town", "Born in the USA", and many others, Bruce Springsteen leaves no doubt about where his heart belongs: it belongs to his family, his friends, his neighborhood, his home town, his country.

These make fine lyrics, one might say. One might even add that those lyrics particularly appeal to dumb, xenophobic, conservative Southerners. Liberals would never confess such lowly belly feelings.

The opposite is true.

Liberals have no idea about the values needed to make their society possible: a society so tolerant that it even accepts intolerant liberals to express their inconsistent opinions.

Among the lyric songwriters, Springsteen is the philosopher of the "common good". The latter concept was invented by the Catholic Church, and rationalized philosophically by Thomas Aquinas. It is a truly "Thomist" concept, although my liberal and retrograde Microsoft Word dictionary erased the term "Thomist". The "common good" is everything that is necessary for a people, tied by common moral values and religion, to live peacefully together.

Springsteen is not a "moral conservative" in the disrespectful sense of someone who opposes all changes whatsoever, but in the excellent sense of someone who opposes all changes toward moral deterioration. In his "the River", he confesses his marriage failure, adducing the adverse economic circumstances at the time, though taking full responsibility of his part of the failure.[43]

As Springsteen's lyrics I chose that of Philadelphia. In that song he criticizes the misery (poverty, hunger, mental problems, homelessness, drug addiction, aids) that thousands were suffering from, in need for a little humanity, but generally left unattended by society.[44]

The video clip[45] is particularly interesting. It shows Bruce walking through South Philadelphia, in an impoverished neighborhood full of garbage-filled vacant lots. As evening falls, poor people warm themselves at improvised hearths. Only ethnic non-Caucasians fill the beautifully taken images. With a single exception: there are two flashes showing famous Hollywood actor Tom Hanks (e.g. Cast Away, by Ridley, 2000), possibly Bruce's soul mate and "South-Philly".

---

[43] By definition, two people are implied in a divorce
[44] Like always, the main institutions taking care of suffering people are Catholic; this also applies to "the Streets of Philadelphia" times of the exploding AIDS epidemics, as shown by history
[45] https://www.youtube.com/watch?v=4z2DtNW79sQ

Streets of Philadelphia
Bruce Springsteen

I was bruised and battered,
I couldn't tell what I felt.
I was unrecognizable to myself.
Saw my reflection in a window
and didn't know my own face.
Oh brother are you gonna leave me wastin' away
On the streets of Philadelphia.
I walked the avenue, 'til my legs felt like stone,
I heard the voices of friends, vanished and gone,
At night I could hear the blood in my veins,
It was just as black and whispering as the rain,
On the streets of Philadelphia.
Ain't no angel gonna greet me.
It's just you and I my friend.
And my clothes don't fit me no more,
A thousand miles
Just to slip this skin.
Night has fallen, I'm lyin' awake,
I can feel myself fading away,
So receive me brother with your faithless kiss,
Or will we leave each other alone like this
On the streets of Philadelphia.

Chaper 15

Bruce is not only a sexy conservative,
he is a hard-core philanthropist, too.
These are one of the many people
whose legacy any society can build its future upon.
A future of love for the philosophical good,
and of tolerance of a maximum acceptable evil.

Chapter 16
Robert Plant

Robert Anthony Plant was born on 20 August 1948, in the Black Country town of West Bromwich, Staffordshire, England, to Robert C. Plant, a qualified civil engineer who worked in the Royal Air Force during the Second World War, and Annie Celia Plant (née Cain), a Romanic woman. He grew up in Kidderminster, Worcestershire. Plant gained an interest in singing and rock and roll music at an early age.[46]

> When I was a kid I used to hide behind the curtains at home at Christmas and I used to try and be Elvis. There was a certain ambience between the curtains and the French windows, there was a certain sound there for a ten-year-old. That was all the ambience I got at ten years old ... I think! And I always wanted to be a curtain, a bit similar to that.

He left King Edward VI Grammar School for Boys in Stourbridge in his mid-teens and developed a strong

---

[46] https://en.wikipedia.org/wiki/Robert_Plant

passion for the blues, mainly through his admiration for Willie Dixon, Robert Johnson and early renditions of songs in this genre.

> I suppose I was quite interested in my stamp collection and Romano-British history. I was a little grammar school boy and I could hear this kind of calling through the airwaves.

He abandoned training as a chartered accountant after only two weeks to attend college in an effort to gain more GCE passes and to become part of the English Midlands blues scene.

> I left home at 16, and I started my real education musically, moving from group to group, furthering my knowledge of the blues and of other music which had weight and was worth listening to".

Plant's early blues influences included Johnson, Bukka White, Skip James, Jerry Miller, and Sleepy John Estes. Plant had various jobs while pursuing his music career, one of which was working for the major British construction company Wimpey in Birmingham in 1967 laying tarmac on roads. He also worked at Woolworth's in Halesowen town for a short period of time. He cut three obscure singles on CBS Records and sang with a variety of bands, including the Crawling King Snakes, which brought him into contact with drummer John Bonham.

They both went on to play in the Band of Joy, merging blues with newer psychedelic trends.

In 1975, Plant and his wife Maureen (now divorced) were seriously injured in a car crash in Rhodes, Greece. This significantly affected the production of Led Zeppelin's seventh album Presence for a few months while he recovered, and forced the band to cancel the remaining tour dates for the year.

In July 1977, his son Karac died at the age of five while Plant was engaged on Led Zeppelin's concert tour of the United States. It was a devastating loss for the family. Plant retreated to his home in the Midlands and for months afterwards he questioned his future. Karac's death later inspired him to write several songs in tribute: "All My Love" featured on Led Zeppelin's final studio album, 1979's In Through the Out Door, while "Blue Train" featured on Page and Plant's second and final (studio) album, 1998's Walking into Clarksdale. The song "I Believe" on Plant's solo album Fate of Nations is another tribute to his late son.

Plant's lyrics with Led Zeppelin were often mystical, philosophical and spiritual, alluding to events in classical and Norse mythology, such as "Immigrant Song", which refers to Valhalla and Viking conquests.[26] However, the song "No Quarter" is often misunderstood to refer to the god Thor; the song actually refers to Mount Thor (which is named after the god). Another example is "The Rain Song".

Plant was also influenced by J. R. R. Tolkien, whose book series inspired lyrics in some early Led Zeppelin songs. Most notably "The Battle of Evermore", "Misty Mountain Hop","No Quarter", "Ramble On" and "Over the Hills and Far Away" contain verses referencing Tolkien's The Lord of the Rings and The Hobbit. [...]

Welsh mythology also forms a basis of Plant's interest in mystical lyrics. He grew up close to the Welsh border and would often take summer trips to Snowdonia. Plant bought a Welsh sheep farm in 1973, and began taking Welsh lessons and looking into the mythology of the land (such as Black Book of Carmarthen, Book of Taliesin, etc.) Plant's first son, Karac, was named after the Welsh warrior Caratacus. The song "Bron-Y-Aur Stomp" is named after the 18th century Welsh cottage Bron-Yr-Aur owned by a friend of his father; it later inspired the song "Bron-Yr-Aur". The songs "Misty Mountain Hop", "That's the Way", and early dabblings in what would become "Stairway to Heaven" were written in Wales and lyrically reflect Plant's mystical view of the land. Critic Steve Turner suggests that Plant's early and continued experiences in Wales served as the foundation for his broader interest in the mythologies he revisits in his lyrics (including those myth systems of Tolkien and the Norse). Page's passion for diverse musical experiences influenced Plant to explore Africa, specifically Marrakesh in Morocco where he encountered Umm Kulthum.

Until here the Wikipedia quote.

Stairway To Heaven
(Led Zeppelin)
Robert Plant[47]

There's a lady who's sure all that glitters is gold
And she's buying a stairway to heaven.
When she gets there she knows, if the stores are all closed
With a word she can get what she came for.
There's a sign on the wall but she wants to be sure
'Cause you know sometimes words have two meanings.
In a tree by the brook, there's a songbird who sings,
Sometimes all of our thoughts are misgiven.

There's a feeling I get when I look to the west,
And my spirit is crying for leaving.
In my thoughts I've seen rings of smoke through the trees,
And the voices of those who stand looking.
And it's whispered that soon, if we all call the tune,
Then the piper will lead us to reason.
And a new day will dawn for those who stand long,
And the forests will echo with laughter.

---

[47] Song Writers: Robert Plant and Jimmy Page
Producer: Jimmy Page, released November 8th, 1971

If there's a bustle in your hedgerow,
don't be alarmed now,
It's just a spring clean for the May queen.
Yes, there are two paths you can go by,
but in the long run there's still time
to change the road you're on.
Your head is humming and it won't go,
In case you don't know, the piper's calling you to join him,
Dear lady, can you hear the wind blow, and did you know
Your stairway lies on the whispering wind?

And as we wind on down the road
Our shadows taller than our soul.
There walks a Lady we all know
Who shines white light and wants to show
How everything still turns to gold.
And if you listen very hard
The tune will come to you at last.
When all are one and one is all
To be a rock and not to roll.

And she's buying a stairway to heaven.

Robert Plant

Just like Paul McCartney, Robert Plant wrote unmistakable lyrics, yet claiming that they are open to interpretation. Just like in Paul's case, nothing is farther from truth in Robert's case. They are both in complete denial syndrome. Why? Because their messages to society are politically incorrect. In order not to incur the public wrath for being politically incorrect, they both found it easier to simply deny the overt meaning of their lyrics.

According to SMF (June 13th, 2019),[48] the four verses can be interpreted in the following sense:

> The first verse is based on the tale of, according to Plant, a materialistic and selfish woman. It is clear that this individual equates "heaven" with shopping. And apparently even if stores are closed, she can still get access to "what she came for" "with a word", insinuating that she is so powerful and wealthy that with just a phone call, the shops will be opened for her.
>
> The second verse is based on Plant envisioning "the west" apparently being destroyed by "rings of smoke" that are visible "through the trees". Again this is something that is occurring only in his thoughts, but still his "spirit is crying for leaving". What geographical region Plant considers "the west" is unspecified, with some even putting forth theories that it refers to the

---

[48]   https://www.songmeaningsandfacts.com/led-zeppelins-stairway-to-heaven-lyrics-meaning/

Wild West. But considering that the song was written in England, the implication would be somewhere west of the United Kingdom. This verse is climaxed by a group of people "who stand" and witness of this fire.

And apparently these same people are referred to in the third verse as "those who stand long". The story being told in this section is that if these individuals have a mutual desire "the piper will lead (them) to reason". And instead of the trees burning now, "the forests echo with laughter". It is never specified who "the piper" actually is, though all things considered, it definitely plays out like a religious reference.

The beginning of the fourth verse brings up the character of the "May queen" and accordingly is about fertility and the advent of Spring. Later the concept of heaven is again brought up though implicitly, as in people having a choice to choose between "two paths" upon which to tread. And once again, "the piper" is present, this time as someone who is "calling you to join him", as in follow the same path that he is on.

Until here SMF's politically correct interpretation. I wish to add a few frustrated remarks of my own.

First of all, for a Welshman living on the coast, the "west" primarily means Ireland, not at all "the Wild West", which only some Americans gone wild can imagine: Those who think of themselves as the navel of the world.

Second, from his youth preference for many Catholic or Catholicizing books, Plant would not particularly sympathize with the age-old Anglican misbehavior towards Catholics, either British or foreign. Consequently, for a Welsh Catholic "the west" is nothing farther than the next island: the once Catholic Ireland. A cold-hearted and rapidly extinguishing Anglican hierarchy goes buried under four centuries of crimes: Torturing native and foreign Catholics, despising a frequently famine-struck country,[49] and[50] most humbly advising Cromwell to have a tiny group of Scottish paranoid Presbyterians settle on stolen Irish property, for the mere sake of creating division. "Who wields the sword shall die by it", the Anglican See might have known, had they spent less time on planning and implementing immorality, and more time on reading Holy Scripture. This Anglican strategy is highly effective, indeed. Roman wisdom called it "divide et impera": Reigning is easier over people who are inner divided by fratricide hatred. I do fear the Anglican See learnt the details of such a

---

[49] located but one hour's boat travel away from the not so Holy Anglican See

[50] when Ireland for once happened not to be devastated by natural catastrophes

strategy from EZ, which has some three millennia of experience in applying it all over the planet.[51]

Third, the piper represents Jesus or one of his prophets: no mystery here. The piper's tune is the Holy Spirit softly stirring our consciences. Equally biblical is Plant's verse that a stairway to heaven cannot be bought with earthly wealth: Remember Jesus' parable of the beggar Lazarus lying at the door of the rich man's house, or his mysterious remark on the impossibility of "rich" people[52] to enter into heaven. This holds the more for a selfish and arrogant lady: That the "stairway to heaven lies on the whispering wind", is likewise, nothing but a remastered quote from John 3,8:

> **The wind bloweth where it will, and thou hearest the sound thereof, but canst not tell whence it cometh and whither it goeth: so is every one that is born of the Spirit."**

Fourth, the May Queen and "the Lady we all know, who shines white light and wants to show how everything still turns to gold" is the Blessed Virgin and Mother of God.

Only the last two sentences are totally out of the ball park: "To be a rock and not to roll" plainly refers to Led

---

[51] This topic is studied in more depth in my decalogue book "The Snake: Three Millennia of Anti-Semitism".

[52] With "rich", Jesus means the combination of wealthy and spiritually self-sufficient

Zeppelin playing "their" rock and roll, which is of a special kind; nowadays known as heavy metal.

*Robert Plant knows that true happiness only comes as the fruit of virtue;
in that fight one may never lower one's guard*

www.ingramcontent.com/pod-product-compliance
Lightning Source LLC
Chambersburg PA
CBHW052105070526
44584CB00017B/2346